EXPLORER BOOKS

BEARS

by Megan Stine

To anyone who has ever loved a grizzly, saved a panda, or stepped aside to let a polar bear pass—to all those who have lowered the muzzles of their guns in admiration and respect for one of nature's most magnificent creatures—this book is dedicated.

Published by The Trumpet Club
666 Fifth Avenue, New York, New York 10103
Copyright © 1993 Parachute Press, Inc.

ISBN 0-440-84139-9
Printed in the United States of America
January 1993
1   3   5   7   9   10   8   6   4   2
CWO

PHOTOGRAPH CREDITS

p. 21: top, © Comstock Inc./Boyd Norton; bottom, © Animals Animals/Robert Maier. p. 22: top, © D. Middleton/SUPERSTOCK; bottom, © Gary Alt. p. 23: top, © Mia & Klaus/SUPERSTOCK; bottom, © Joy A. Guravich/Photo Researchers. p. 24: top, © M. Roessler/SUPERSTOCK; bottom, © Animals Animals/Michael Dick. p. 25: top, © Gary Alt; bottom, © Comstock Inc./Russ Kinne. p. 26: top, © SUPERSTOCK; bottom, © Animals Animals/Margot Conte. p. 27: top, © Gary Alt; bottom, © Comstock Inc./Townsend Dickinson. p. 28: top, © Gary Alt; bottom, © Alan Carey/Photo Researchers.

Cover: © Will Regan/International Stock

Contents

Introduction

One night in May 1987, an 11-year-old boy named Juan Perez made a terrible mistake. He climbed into a cage with the polar bears at the Prospect Park Zoo in Brooklyn, New York. Juan lived near the zoo, and he had seen the polar bears before. They looked pretty tame to him. They hardly ever growled at onlookers, and they acted friendly when the zookeepers fed them. So when Juan's friends dared him to climb into the cage, he agreed to do it. But within a few minutes, two of the bears mauled him to death.

Of course, everyone was horrified by the tragic accident. But it's easy to understand what went wrong. Juan had made the deadly mistake of thinking that the bears were as gentle as they looked.

Juan isn't the only person who doesn't understand bear behavior. Lots of people are confused about it. We don't know whether to love bears—or run from them. Some bears look like great big cuddly versions of teddy bears. Who wouldn't want to snuggle up with a cute, chubby giant panda in a zoo?

But some bears are known killers. Grizzly bears have attacked and killed hikers in Yellowstone National Park. And black bears are constantly barging into campers' tents.

No wonder we don't know whether to befriend bears—or to beware!

What are bears really like? Are they cuddlers or killers? The truth is somewhere in between. Bears are very complex animals. They are extremely intelligent and shy—but also stubborn, fierce, and unpredictable. They usually stay away from humans, but some bears are so used to people that they even go swimming in backyard pools! Mother bears are gentle and loving to their cubs—but fathers are loners that sometimes kill the cubs. Bears walk slowly and look clumsy, but they can outrun and kill a galloping horse!

There are eight *species,* or kinds, of bears in the world. (See the table on page 10.) And they come in many sizes and colors. The three that live in North America are the American black bear, the brown bear (the grizzly is a kind of brown bear), and the polar bear (found in all arctic regions, including those in Canada and Alaska). There are more bears in North America than in any other place on earth, but bears live all over the globe. In fact, every continent except Africa and Australia has some kind of bear. (If you're wondering about koalas, they aren't bears. They're *marsupials,* a class of animals in which the mother as a rule carries her babies in her pouch. Other marsupials include opossums and kangaroos.)

The other five species of bears in the world are

quite rare. Have you ever heard of the spectacled bear of South America? Or the sloth bear? Or the Asian black bear? And then there's the smallest bear in the world, the sun bear. Hardly anyone has ever seen a sun bear, except in zoos. In the wild, they are so rare that even scientists have a hard time finding them.

Last but not least comes a fun-to-watch bear—the giant panda. For many years scientists thought that these animals weren't really bears at all. They don't eat meat, they don't sleep for long periods of time, and they don't roar, as other bears do. Since giant pandas don't act like bears, scientists thought they must not *be* bears. Some experts even thought that giant pandas might be related to raccoons.

But in 1985 a researcher named Stephen O'Brien performed a number of tests on pandas. He compared the blood and DNA of pandas with that of other bears. *DNA* is the basic genetic material of life. It is like a code that carries all the information about an animal's physical traits and characteristics. The results proved once and for all that giant pandas really are bears and not cousins of raccoons!

So welcome to the world of bears. Once you learn more about these fascinating animals, you'll never confuse a real bear with Winnie-the-Pooh again!

1

Just the Bear Facts

All bears are *mammals,* animals that are warm-blooded, have a backbone, and have hair on their skin. Mammals nurse their young with milk from the mother's *mammary glands,* or breasts. Bears take care of their babies much longer than most other animals do. Bear cubs stay with their mothers for at least a year, and sometimes as long as 2 or 3 years. During that time, bear mothers raise their young, called *cubs,* and teach them how to survive.

Like most people, bears are *omnivores.* That means that they eat both meat and plants. Bears also walk like people, placing their whole foot flat on the ground. Scientists call this way of walking *plantigrade.*

But when it comes to the feet themselves, bears' feet are nothing like yours. Not unless you wear a size 22 shoe and have great big curving claws! Bears have big feet, and they use their claws for digging holes and attacking their *prey,* the animals they kill to eat. Usually the claws on a bear's hind feet are longer than the ones on its front feet. When a bear gets into a fight with another big animal, it can hold the animal with its front feet and use its back claws

4

to attack. Unlike a cat's claws, bear claws can't be *retracted,* or pulled in.

Bears walk and run on all fours most of the time. They usually stand up on their hind feet only to look around—and sniff around—or to scare you! You've probably seen pictures of a grizzly bear standing on its hind legs, with its teeth bared, lips curled, and claws extended. It looks pretty terrifying in that position, doesn't it? Well, that's the whole idea. Bears stand up to threaten other animals and scare them away. But they don't launch an attack while standing up. When a bear is ready to charge, it drops to all fours. That's when an angry bear is the most dangerous!

If you look at the tracks of a running bear, you'll discover one other fact about bear feet. The toes of each foot are turned toward those of the opposite foot. Bears are *pigeon-toed!*

Small Eyes, Big Nose, Long Teeth

Bears are *predators,* animals that hunt other animals for food. That means they've got to have the right equipment to find and kill their prey.

The right equipment in a bear's case is smack in the middle of its face. It's a super-sniffer nose. A grizzly bear can smell as keenly as a bloodhound. That is, a grizzly can follow the trail of a person or an animal just by sniffing the ground where the prey walked. Grizzly bears can also detect the smell of food on the clothing people wore when they were cooking at a campsite. If you sleep in those clothes, the scent will lead the bear right to your tent! Polar bears can do the same thing.

For years, scientists thought that bears had poor vision. Why? For one thing, bears have small eyes. Also, when bear researchers went out into the wild to observe bears, the animals often looked away. Experts thought this meant that the bears just couldn't see them well. But after more careful observation, scientists realized that the bears were ignoring them on purpose. It's the bear's way of saying, "I'm not looking, so just get going. I'll let you get out of my way." Scientists now have a name for this bear strategy. They call it *ignoring behavior.*

If a bear decides *not* to ignore you, watch out! Bears can do a lot of damage in a very short time. Not only are their paws and claws powerful, but bears also have canine teeth that they use to bite, hold, and kill their prey. *Canine teeth* are the long, pointed teeth on each side of each jaw. An older bear will have especially long canine teeth because a bear's teeth keep growing throughout its life. The older the bear, the bigger its teeth! Scientists can tell how old a bear is by removing one of its teeth and slicing through it. The tooth has growth rings, like the rings in a tree that tell the tree's age.

Mama, Papa, and Baby Bears

Picture a 200-pound adult panda. What size do you think the baby panda will be? Amazingly, a giant panda has a baby that weighs only 3 ounces. That's about the size of a candy bar!

Giant pandas are not the smallest bears, but they have the tiniest babies. Other bears have very small babies, too. Polar bears are huge—some of them weigh almost a ton—but their babies weigh only about 20 ounces. That's about the size of a large grapefruit!

Most bears mate in the spring. The females are pregnant for 5 to 8 months. The babies are usually born the following winter, while the mothers are in their dens.

If the mother is sick or food is scarce, the cub does not develop in the *womb,* the place in the mother's body where a baby grows. That way the mother won't have to raise a family when she isn't able to take care of it.

While bear cubs stay with their mothers, the papa bears are nowhere in sight. Adult males and females almost never spend time together—except for a few weeks when they're mating. After that the fathers leave. This is probably for the best; adult male bears are a threat to the cubs. Many cubs die when males attack and eat them.

Long Snooze

How long do you think you could sleep without changing your position? One hour? Five hours? All night? Well, no matter what your answer is, it's nothing compared to a bear. Even if you slept for a solid

24 hours after a sleepover, you'd never be able to "outsleep" a bear. Why not? Because you don't hibernate.

Hibernation is the behavior that some animals use to spend the winter in a deep sleep. During true hibernation, an animal's body temperature drops significantly, and the animal cannot be awakened easily. Chipmunks and other small mammals hibernate this way.

Bears sleep through much of the winter, too, but scientists question whether a bear's winter sleep can be called true hibernation. A bear's body temperature doesn't drop much when it's sleeping. It goes down only about 9 degrees. Also, the bear can be easily awakened.

Whether it is true hibernation or not, a bear's winter sleep is a long one. Some bears stay in their dens for 7 months—more than half the year. And some bears sleep for as long as a month without moving an inch!

When a bear is in its winter den, many of the animal's body functions slow down. Sleeping bears don't eat, and they don't *urinate* or *defecate,* which means they don't "go to the bathroom." And their heart rate slows down a lot, too. Just the same, a sleeping bear burns up about 4,000 calories per day. That's why bears need to eat a lot before they enter their winter dens. Grizzly bears can lose almost 200 pounds by simply doing nothing all winter.

Why do bears sleep all winter in the first place? Are they just lazy? No way. Northern bears enter their dens in the fall because they know that winter is coming and the food supply will be low. Without food, the bear would not have enough energy to go about its normal life. So the animal sleeps through most of the harsh winter months to conserve energy. When spring comes and the food supply is again plentiful, the bear wakes up.

The length of a bear's winter sleep depends on the length of winter. Some bears sleep for only 2 or 3 months. Bears in harsh climates den much longer— for as long as 7 months. When bears *den,* they find a place to sleep in an enclosed space. A good den is a cave, a rotten log, or a hollow tree. But bears living in warm climates don't sleep for long periods. Neither do zoo bears—even the ones in cold climates. Zoo bears usually remain active all winter because they are fed constantly.

For some reason, once in a while an individual grizzly bear or black bear just can't seem to get to sleep! It doesn't sleep for long periods at all, even though the other bears in the species do. Maybe these bears are just like people who like stay up all night. Or maybe they were just born to prowl!

THE EIGHT BEARS OF THE WORLD

SPECIES (Some subspecies are listed under the species name.)	WHERE THEY LIVE
AMERICAN BLACK BEAR KERMODE	North America British Columbia (Canada)

BROWN BEAR
 	
  GRIZZLY
  KODIAK
  EUROPEAN BROWN BEAR
	North America, Europe, Asia, Japan, India, the former Soviet Union
	United States and Canada
	Alaska
	Europe

POLAR BEAR	All arctic regions, including those in Alaska, Canada, Russia, Norway, and Greenland
GIANT PANDAS	Tibetan Plateau of China
SUN BEAR	Asia and Malaysia
ASIAN BLACK BEAR (also called MOON BEAR)	Much of Asia, including China, Japan, Iran, Bangladesh, Pakistan, Laos
SPECTACLED BEAR	Andes Mountains of South America
SLOTH BEAR	India, Sri Lanka, Nepal

2

American Bears: From Grizzlies to Teddies

It was August, and school would be starting soon. Two 8th-grade boys, Mike Moerlein and Scott Mac-Innes, were camping in Alaska by themselves. They were out looking for moose, because the moose hunting season was about to begin. But the boys weren't hunting. The only weapons they had with them were slingshots.

One morning, as they walked toward a valley, they saw a bear footprint. It wasn't very big, according to Mike, and it was pointed in the opposite direction from the way they were walking. So the boys weren't too worried. But a short time later, they heard a terrible growl. "Moose!" Mike yelled, thinking that a big bull moose was charging them. It took only a few seconds for him to realize that it wasn't a moose. It was a grizzly bear!

Mike hid behind a tree, but Scott started running. The bear immediately attacked Scott. When Mike saw what was happening, he knew he had to do something to save his friend, so he tried to distract the bear. He jumped out from behind the tree, waved his arms, and then shot the bear with his slingshot.

11

The trick worked!—for a minute. It got the bear to leave Scott alone. But suddenly, the grizzly charged Mike, biting him on the hip and the head. Then the bear went back to bite Scott one more time before it left.

In spite of getting some wounds, the boys were lucky. They had survived a grizzly bear attack. But why had the bear attacked in the first place? That was a mystery to them then, and it still is now.

When it comes to *grizzly bears,* there's one thing that bear experts agree on: Grizzlies are unpredictable. But once you get to know more about the animals, you can begin to understand what makes them attack—and how to avoid being hurt.

First things first: Let's get the names straight. Grizzlies are a *subspecies,* or type, of brown bear. *Brown bears* are found all over the northern part of the world. But grizzlies are found only in North America. It's the special name given to all brown bears living *inland* (not near the coast) in the United States and Canada.

The other kind of brown bear found in North America is the *Kodiak bear,* named for Kodiak Island in southern Alaska where it lives. Kodiak bears are huge—more than 9 feet tall. Large males can weigh 1,800 pounds, or almost a ton!

But brown bears aren't the only species of bear found in the United States. The other species is called the *American black bear.* American black bears are strictly American. That is, they're not found anywhere else in the world *except* North America. And black bears have one other claim to fame: The first teddy bear was based on a black bear cub!

It happened in 1903 when Theodore "Teddy" Roosevelt was president. One day, on a hunting trip, President Roosevelt refused to shoot a little American black bear cub. Soon after that, a toy company made a small stuffed bear for children and named it the "Teddy" bear.

Today, almost half a million black bears roam the American countryside. These bears usually live in forests, but not always far from people. In fact, the bears of Yellowstone National Park are visited by an average of about 25,000 people every day. American black bears outnumber all the other bears of the world *combined*. Fewer than 1,000 brown bears remain in the continental United States. They live in only four states: Wyoming, Montana, Idaho, and Washington. In Canada and Alaska, though, the grizzly, the brown bear subspecies, is thriving, with more than 40,000 living there in the wild.

What's in a Name?

Before you get to know the bears of America any better, let's clear up one more thing. Brown bears aren't always brown. And American black bears aren't always black. In fact, both bears come in both colors! So what's going on with these names?

The truth is that the common names for bears are often confusing. To clarify matters, each species is given a Latin name as well. In Latin, a grizzly bear is called *Ursus arctos horribilis. Ursus* is the Latin word for "bear." *Arctos* means "northern." And *horribilis* is a Latin version of just what it sounds like—"horrible"!

Other brown bears are called *Ursus arctos,* too. But they have a different last name. For instance, the Kodiak's Latin name is *ursus arctos middendorffi!* (Aleksandr Fiodorovich Middendorff was a German naturalist who lived from 1815 to 1894.)

Comparing Bears

What are the differences between black bears and brown bears—and how can you tell them apart if you meet one in the woods?

The easiest way to compare American bears is to start with size. Black bears are smaller than brown bears. The average black bear weighs between 350 and 600 pounds, and males are larger than females. Black bears stand about 6 feet tall on hind legs, and about 3 feet tall on all fours. By comparison, brown bears tower over black bears in both weight and height. An average male brown bear weighs about 700 pounds. Some of them have even topped 1,000 pounds—almost half the size of a small car! Big brown bears such as grizzlies can stand 8 feet tall on their hind legs. And here's the really scary part: Male brown bears continue to grow throughout their lives. So the older a male bear gets, the bigger he grows.

Of course, since black bears come in most of the

same colors that brown bears do, you can't tell whether a bear is a black bear or a brown bear by its color alone. Most often, however, black bears are black. But they can also be brown, or a reddish-brown color called cinnamon. The important thing to remember is this: A black bear's coat is always glossy or shiny. A brown bear's fur coat never is.

What other colors do black bears come in? Believe it or not, white! The white version of the black bear is a subspecies called the *Kermode bear*. It's found only in a small coastal area of British Columbia in Canada. Kermodes aren't always white. They can be cream, yellow, orange, or even a bluish-gray.

Kermodes are so rare that few people have ever seen them. Maybe that's why the local people have a special name for the Kermode bear. They call it the "ghost bear."

Brown bears come in brown, black, red, cinnamon, blond, and various mixtures, including "grizzly." Grizzly coats are dark brown with silver-tipped hairs. Grizzly bears are named after this grizzled, or streaked, coat color that many of them have.

Okay, so you're walking in the woods and you suddenly see a bear. It's not huge, and its fur is brownish-black. You can't tell whether the fur is glossy or not—you're too scared to remember about that anyway. So is there another way to tell if it's a brown bear?

Yes. There are two distinct physical differences between black bears and brown ones. Brown bears have long, visible claws. But the claws on a black bear probably won't show very much. And brown bears have a shoulder hump. Sticking up just behind the neck, the hump is a dead giveaway to all forms of brown bear. The body of a black bear, by comparison, makes a smooth, flat line from head to tail when the bear is on all fours.

But the most important difference between a black bear and a brown is the personality. Black bears are naturally afraid of people. They'll usually run and hide from danger—and that includes humans—unless they've lost their fear of people through repeated contacts.

Brown bears, on the other hand, are fearless and much more aggressive than blacks. If a brown bear is surprised or feels threatened, it'll stay and fight. Black bears are sometimes scared away, but brown bears aren't.

Where's the Bear?

Where, exactly, do bears like to live? That's an easy one. Where did Goldilocks find the Three Bears? The woods, of course. Anywhere you find hardwood forests or large stands of pine trees, you're likely to find bears. Most of the black bears in the United States live in the northern forests of the East and the West. Grizzlies prefer mountainous woods with river valleys for fishing. They also like to have a meadow nearby, full of wildflowers and tasty berries.

Unlike the Three Bears, however, real bears don't

sit in chairs or sleep in beds. They prefer to sleep on a pile of leaves in a den.

Breakfast of Champions

Black and brown bears will eat anything. They're not too picky. Grass, berries, termites, honey, fruit, fish, dead animal flesh, or sometimes people—it doesn't matter. It's all tasty to bears. Especially the honey! That's one of their favorite foods. Black bears love honey and will tear open a beehive to get at it, even if it means getting stung. The main thing a bear really cares about is the nutritional value of the food. Why? Because the bear knows that its summers are short and the winters are long. In order to survive the winter, a grizzly must fatten up by putting away about 80 or 90 pounds of food per day.

In the wild, both black bears and brown bears eat mostly plants because these are usually the easiest food to find. Amazingly, bears have an ability to sense which plants are most nutritious. And they'll eat these plants only when they're highest in protein —right before the plant flowers.

Alaskan brown and black bears are a little different because they live in a land of plenty. Plenty of what? Salmon! Each year, the bears wait eagerly for the time when salmon begin swimming upstream. Then these expert fishermen go to work. They scoop the salmon right out of the water with their paws. Or they "snorkel" for salmon by dipping their heads under water and waiting for a fish to swim by. In fish-

17

ing, too, bears can tell which fish have the highest protein content. If there are plenty of salmon, bears will eat only the richest part of the fish—the brain and skin, for instance, or the eggs of a female salmon.

Bears on Vacation

People love to vacation in our national parks. These are great places to picnic and camp out under the stars. There's only one problem: Campers bring food—hamburgers, hot dogs, and pies. And bears have a keen sense of smell that leads them to food—and campsites.

The result is that bears go on vacation, too. They stop *foraging,* or searching for food from natural sources. Instead, they live on human garbage. They hang out at the garbage dumps in the parks, chowing down on what amounts to junk food for bears. Or worse—they raid the campsites while the campers are still there!

People camping in bear country are warned never to leave food around. Once a meal has been cooked and eaten, all the leftover food should be wrapped tightly, then stored in a locked car or hung from a tree, out of a bear's reach. The farther from the tents and campsite, the better. If the food is wrapped tightly enough, the bear shouldn't be able to smell it. But just in case, the food should be stored far away from the tents, and out of reach. That way, if a bear comes, it won't come into your tent, and it won't be able to eat your food. Smart campers put everything —even the clothes they wear while cooking—into an airtight plastic cooler.

By nature, most bears—especially black bears— would just as soon avoid people. But the park bears are just the opposite. They've gotten used to seeing people everywhere they look. Black bears in Yellowstone beg for food, and sometimes visitors and campers feed them—which is a big mistake. Bears are smart and they learn quickly. Feeding them just teaches them that people are a good source of food.

Although park bears may seem friendly, they're really not tame at all. In fact, they're more dangerous than bears in the wild. They've learned that humans are not much of a threat, so they have no fear of forcing themselves on humans.

Countdown to Extinction

In Yellowstone National Park, park rangers count and keep track of the brown bears. To do this, they give the bears a kind of personal bear ID. After all, you can't ask to see a bear's driver's license! So scientists have come up with a safe system for labeling each bear.

First, park rangers must capture the bears and put them to sleep with a *tranquilizer dart gun,* a gun that shoots a drug into an animal to immobilize it safely and temporarily. Then an ear tag with a number on it is put on each bear. Some bears are given *radio collars.* These collars send out a signal that can be *tracked,* or followed. That way, bear researchers can follow the movements and habits of individual bears.

At last count, there were only about 230 grizzlies in Yellowstone. That's a pretty small number—so small, in fact, that Yellowstone grizzlies are considered threatened with extinction. *Threatened* is an official term for an animal that isn't yet endangered, but is getting close to it. An *endangered* animal is one that is near extinction. It is against the law to shoot a threatened or endangered animal, or to destroy its *habitat,* the area where the animal lives.

Actually, grizzlies are about as rare in the continental United States as giant pandas are in the world. But for some reason, not as many people want to protect the grizzly from extinction.

A grizzly bear named Rollie lives with two of her cubs at the McNeil River Sanctuary in Alaska.

Two European brown bears in Germany wrestle playfully.

Three Alaskan brown bears dive into turbulent water in search of salmon.

On a successful fishing expedition, an Alaskan brown bear rips apart its salmon catch with its teeth.

Never get close to a polar bear. This Canadian bear looks cute but will attack if disturbed.

A polar bear mother relaxes with her two 8-month-old cubs.

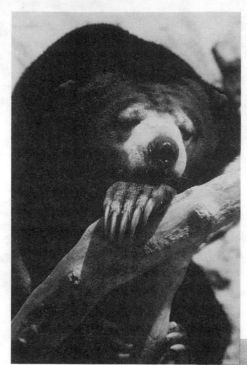

The sun bear, a rare Asian bear, is the smallest kind of bear in the world. It likes to sleep in trees during the day.

The sloth bear uses its long muzzle to suck termites out of their nests in the forests of India and Sri Lanka.

The spectacled bear, a shaggy black bear from the Andes Mountains of South America, is easily identified by the golden markings on its face.

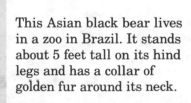

This Asian black bear lives in a zoo in Brazil. It stands about 5 feet tall on its hind legs and has a collar of golden fur around its neck.

These three giant pandas spend much of their time eating bamboo. They each consume between 50 and 85 pounds a day!

The huge Kodiak bear, named for its home—Kodiak Island in southern Alaska—can weigh almost a ton and reach a height of 9 feet.

Two curious adult American black bears pose for the camera.

Bear alert! An American black bear raids a picnic table in California.

Some 2-month-old American black bear cubs make their way out of a tree trunk den.

An American black bear cub in western Montana learns how to climb a tree.

3

Polar Bears: Ice Is Nice

The temperature in New York City dropped to a bone-chilling 12°F one morning. Everyone was shivering. Even the lions, tigers, and bears at the zoo were shivering in their fur coats. But wait a minute. The bears? Well—maybe the brown bears were cold. But not the polar bears! They looked as happy as they could be.

Two polar bears jumped up, full of energy, and began playing with each other. They leaped from rock to rock in their cage, obviously feeling great even though it was well below freezing outside. This was their idea of a beautiful day!

Polar bears can survive quite happily in temperatures that would turn other beings into solid ice. In the Arctic regions—such as those in Russia, Canada, Norway, and Greenland—where polar bears live most of the year, the ground is frozen solid. (Polar bears don't live very close to the North Pole, however, because few seals, the bears' favorite food, or any other animals live that far north.) Temperatures can drop to –60°F. But the bears are dressed for the cold. Their skin is actually black, which helps to absorb sunlight. Their fur is so thick, however, that it hides the black skin. The fur appears to be white but is actually made of clear hollow hairs. Because the hairs are hollow, they catch the sun's rays and direct the heat right to the bear's skin.

Polar bears have two other characteristics that help them survive in the cold. One is a thick layer of fat—about 4 inches of it. The other is that they have fur on every inch of their bodies except their noses. They even have fur on their feet to help keep them from slipping on the ice!

What's for Dinner? Seals Again!

Technically, polar bears are omnivores. But even though they'll eat both meat and plants, let's face it: There aren't too many vegetables growing on the ice of the Arctic Circle! And a polar bear's digestive system isn't really designed to handle a lot of *roughage,* or coarse, bulky food. Polar bears wouldn't do well on an all-salad diet. If the food supply is good, polar bears eat seals, walruses, and fish.

To hunt seals, a bear must stay near the edge of the polar ice, where the ice meets the sea. That's where the seals live, so that's prime territory for polar bears, too. The biggest male bears always take the best hunting spots because they're *dominant*— they're powerful enough to chase other bears away. Then come the females with cubs, followed by the females without cubs and the younger animals. So if you're a small polar bear without much rank in the community, you've got to stay well back from the best seal-hunting territory.

Polar bears have a keenly developed sense of smell. They can smell a seal from 20 miles away! And they have several special hunting techniques for catching their prey. Sometimes, if a seal is sitting on the ice, a bear will float along in the water next to it. The bear remains motionless, pretending to be another big piece of ice. Then all of a sudden the bear will leap from the water in a surprise attack. With one powerful bite of its jaw, the bear can capture and kill the seal.

When the bear is on the ice and the seal is in the water, the polar bear uses a different approach. Sometimes the bear will find a small opening in the ice—a breathing hole for the seal. When the seal comes up for a breath of air, the bear grabs its nose with its teeth. *Chomp!* Then the bear pulls the seal out through the small hole. The seal is dead by the time it's been yanked up.

An average seal weighs between 100 and 200 pounds. The average 1,200-pound male polar bear can eat up to 150 pounds of seal in one sitting. In winter, which is seal season, polar bears eat a whole seal every 5 or 6 days. But at other times of the year, when food is scarce, they can go for weeks without eating.

Polar bears are great swimmers because their front paws are huge, like paddles. Also, their toes are *webbed,* or connected to each other. And since polar bears have such a nice thick coat, they don't mind the icy-cold water. They can swim underwater, submerged to about 15 feet, and stay under for 2 whole minutes without coming up for air. When they do come up and step onto the ice, they shake themselves off like wet dogs.

Winter Walkers

Most polar bears don't actually hibernate. They don't even spend much time in a winter den. For one thing, winter is the time when seals are plentiful. Unlike brown and black bears, who put on weight in the summer and fall, polar bears find their best food supplies in the winter. So polar bears can't afford to sleep just because it's cold. Instead, they just keep walking, constantly walking, prowling the ice for food.

There are two exceptions, though. One is pregnant females and mothers with year-old cubs. They den in snowbanks in the winter to protect their babies from the cold. While denning, the mothers don't eat. They just live on their fat. The other exception is when it's *really, really* cold outside. At temperatures such as −60°F or −70°F, many bears take cover. They'll construct temporary dens by digging a small space in the snow.

Polar Bear Capital of the World

One town in Canada has more polar bear visitors than any other town in the world. It's Churchill,

Manitoba, on the western shore of Canada's Hudson Bay.

Why do the bears come to Churchill in the fall? It all starts in the spring, when the ice of northern Hudson Bay begins to break up and melt. All winter the polar bears have been living on the ice of the bay. Now they ride on large pieces of broken ice, called *floes.* The ice floes land on the southern shore of Hudson Bay. When summer comes, it's too warm for the bears, so they start *migrating,* or moving, north. They walk for about 800 miles until they reach a spot where they know the bay will soon freeze again. That spot just happens to be Churchill.

By this time it's October and the bay isn't yet quite frozen. So the bears simply make themselves at home! They forage for food in garbage dumps or just hang out near the water. Sometimes the bears come too close to town. Then they are captured and marked with giant letters spraypainted in black on their white coats. That way town officials can keep track of nuisance bears. Sometimes the bears have to "get out of town." They're airlifted out by helicopter, to protect the town's residents.

Tourists come to Churchill in October and November to see the town's famous bears. There, visitors can take a guided tour of polar bear country. *Tundra buggies*—huge vehicles on giant-size wheels—prowl the ice looking for polar bears. Tourists ride safely many feet above the ground.

Everyone in Churchill loves the town's mascot animal, but everyone also knows that polar bears are dangerous. Since polar bears spend their whole lives as predators, their hunting and killing skills are sharp. That makes them more dangerous than any other arctic animal—and sometimes more dangerous than any other kind of bear.

In the long run, however, we don't have much to fear from polar bears. Actually it's the other way around. People have killed far more polar bears than bears have killed people. Eskimos, for example, use the meat for food and the fur to make clothing.

Some experts believe that too many polar bears are killed in Canada, causing their numbers to decrease too rapidly. Laws protecting polar bears are helping to stop the killing of these animals. Native peoples in Canada may hunt a total of only 600 to 700 annually, and no one is allowed to hunt the bears from helicopters. Today there are 20,000 to 40,000 polar bears left.

Worldwide, these bears are not considered endangered. Like Canada, the United States and Greenland allow hunting by native peoples who actually use polar bear products for their survival. No polar bear hunting is allowed in Norway and Russia.

4

Panda Power

Imagine a time when no one outside of China had ever seen a *giant panda*. People had heard about the great white and black bears, and they had seen giant panda *pelts,* or skins. But people in America couldn't imagine how appealing real live pandas would be.

In 1936, a wealthy American woman named Ruth Harkness left New York City and sailed for China. She was hunting for giant pandas—but not to kill them. She wanted to capture the first live panda and bring it back to the United States.

Ruth Harkness's husband had gone to China earlier looking for giant pandas, but he had died trying. Now she was taking up her husband's cause.

Mrs. Harkness knew, however, that she couldn't find the bears herself. It was difficult to reach the remote areas where pandas lived, and only native Chinese knew where to look. But finally, after several weeks of trekking through the snow-covered mountains, she reached her goal. The Chinese guides found a tiny 1-month-old giant panda cub. It was so small, a man could hold it in the palms of his hands!

Mrs. Harkness treated the baby panda as if it were

her own child. Day and night she fed it powdered milk mixed with water from a bottle, and as she held it in her arms to keep it warm, it chewed on her sleeve. The cub grew quickly to the size of a teddy bear. When Mrs. Harkness and the adorable panda arrived back in the United States, they became celebrities overnight.

Eventually Mrs. Harkness sold the giant panda to the Brookfield Zoo in Chicago. The bear was named Su Lin. But sadly, Su Lin died within a year. Several other baby pandas were brought out of China, but many of them died quickly, too.

Slowly everyone began to realize that giant pandas are very special animals. They need special treatment. And there was still much to learn about keeping and breeding them in captivity.

Meet the Giant Panda

Giant pandas, called pandas for short, are probably one of the most popular animals in the world. They have an incredible power—the power to attract attention. But attention is the last thing that giant pandas want. Why? Because they are one of the most *solitary* animals on earth. That means they prefer to be alone. They don't even want to spend time with each other! In the wild, pandas go out of their way to avoid each other. There are only two exceptions—during mating season, and when a mother has a cub.

For a few weeks each spring, when the females are

ready to mate, they spend time with male pandas. Then they go off by themselves again. In the fall a cub is born. It is the tiniest of all newborn bears, weighing only 3 or 4 ounces.

Luckily, the tiny panda cub is in good hands—or rather paws—because giant pandas make excellent mothers. They pick their babies up and hold them close. They lick their babies tenderly. And they gently carry them in their mouths, just like mother cats do with their kittens. A giant panda mother almost never leaves her cub alone when it's young. She cradles it close to her day and night. She even takes it with her when she leaves the den to find food or to urinate.

It's amazing to see a 200- to 300-pound panda cuddling with a baby the size of a doughnut! But panda mothers know how fragile their cubs are. At birth the babies are blind and almost hairless. But within a few weeks, the black and white markings begin to appear. Still, the giant panda cubs are helpless. They can't even crawl until they're 2 months old. And they need their mother's milk until they're 5 or 6 months old. Only then do they finally learn to eat what all pandas live on—bamboo.

Young pandas stay with their mothers through two winters, or until they are about 1½ years old. Then it's off to find a good patch of bamboo and start living the lonely life of the panda—until the panda reaches 5 or 6 years of age. Then it is *mature,* or grown up enough, to mate and have panda babies of its own.

Panda Talk

Newborn pandas cry a lot to get their mother's attention, though the cubs eventually outgrow this behavior. And pandas that are ready to mate make chirping and barking noises to attract each other. But other than that, giant pandas are almost silent. They don't growl or roar.

But does that mean giant pandas don't communicate with each other? Not at all. They leave messages for each other by *scent-marking* trees. To mark a tree this way, a panda rubs its rear end against the bark. Pandas have glands on their rear ends that produce a kind of panda "perfume." Some of the scent stays on the tree after the rubbing. Other pandas can smell the scent, and they know what the message means. It says, "Panda in the neighborhood. Watch out—or we might run into each other!" Of course, during mating season, the message is read differently. It says, "Panda in the neighborhood. Anybody home?"

Please Pass the Bamboo

Bamboo, bamboo, and more bamboo! That's all a panda wants—for breakfast, lunch, and dinner. But since bamboo isn't very nutritious, giant pandas have to eat giant-size portions of it in order to survive. In fact, they eat between 50 and 85 pounds of bamboo *every day*. That equals about 1/3 of their body weight. That's like your eating 100 bananas every day!

Eating so much bamboo takes a lot of time and energy. So pandas sleep a lot when they're not munching their favorite food. But they don't sleep through the night. (And they don't hibernate.) Instead, they just take naps between meals. They are good tree climbers, and enjoy napping in trees. It's just eat and sleep, eat and sleep, 24 hours a day.

Since pandas spend so much time eating bamboo, it's a good thing they have special paws. Their paws have a sixth digit that allows them to grasp and hold the food. In truth, it's not really a finger or a thumb. It's a wristbone that can swivel around and be used like a thumb.

There's only one problem with living on an all-bamboo diet: What do pandas do when the bamboo runs out? Most of the time, pandas don't have that problem. They live in an area that's abundant with bamboo. In fact, the mountainsides are covered with it. But once every 40 years or so, an amazing thing happens. The bamboo suddenly flowers and then dies. It takes another 10 years for a good supply of bamboo to grow back again from seed.

Of course, when all the bamboo dies, giant pandas go hungry. That's what happened in 1983. A certain kind of bamboo died, and more than 130 pandas starved to death. Why didn't they move to another area where there was another kind of bamboo? Hundreds of years ago that's probably what the pandas would have done. But now the panda habitats are surrounded by farms. Surrounded by these human settlements, the pandas have nowhere to go.

In captivity, giant pandas will eat meat if it's offered to them. But in the wild, they just don't have what it takes to be a predator. For one thing, there aren't many prey animals in panda territory. So to live on prey animals, pandas would have to roam over a wide area. But giant pandas don't have the energy for such movement. And they don't have the speed to capture prey, either. Pandas move too slowly and clumsily.

Panda experts aren't sure what to do about the growing shortage of bamboo. But everyone agrees that it is one of the reasons that giant pandas are now endangered.

Save the Pandas

There are only about 700 pandas remaining in the wild. That's a very small number considering the fact that females can raise only one baby every 2 or 3 years. What's worse, the panda's natural habitat is slowly being destroyed. People are worried about the future of pandas.

Fortunately, the Chinese government is working hard to protect pandas. They have set aside twelve *panda reserves,* separate areas in the wild for pandas. If you're wondering who decided where the reserves should be, it wasn't the government. It was the pandas! Each reserve is a small area where pandas are naturally found. Some reserves have only about 10 pandas living in them, but others have as many as 150. In Wolong reserve, the largest, there is also a panda research station. Wolong is located in the mountains of China's Sichuan Province.

Right now no one is sure just how to increase the panda population. Pandas don't always breed well in captivity, especially outside of China. In Mexico, Japan, and Spain, some females have managed to breed well. But the babies born in captivity can't be released into the pandas' natural habitat because no one knows whether they could survive in the wild.

Maybe the best way to save the pandas is to make sure that they have plenty of natural habitat. People can try to preserve the forests they live in. In addition, we can make sure they have the two things they like best in all the world: bamboo and privacy.

5

Rare Bears

How would you like to see some of the smallest, rarest bears in the world? No problem. There are two places you can go. One place is Borneo, an island in the South Pacific. Airfare from California: about $2,000. The other place is much closer and much less expensive to get to—especially if you live in California. It has an admission fee of only about $12—it's the San Diego Zoo!

The *sun bear* is a small, unusual-looking creature that roams through the forests of Asia, Malaysia, and, possibly, India. It is the smallest bear in the world, weighing no more than 100 pounds as an adult and standing only 4 1/2 feet tall. It is also the rarest bear in the world. Few wildlife researchers have ever even been able to *find* the sun bear in the wild. That's why your best chance to see one is probably a visit to the San Diego Zoo.

Of course, in a zoo you won't see the sun bear doing what it does best—scampering over the forest floor, foraging for food. According to Terry Domico, a wildlife writer and photographer who followed a sun bear through the forest, these bears move quickly. They almost never stop hunting for food. They just keep nibbling on little snacks as they go.

In the wild, sun bears eat fruit, rodents, bees, eggs, termites, worms, lizards, and some plants. And like almost all bears, they also *love* honey. The sun bear is fearless in attacking beehives.

And speaking of fearless, the sun bear is pretty tough on other animals, too. It has a reputation for being one of the most aggressive animals in the forest. Sometimes it attacks for no apparent reason.

Why is the sun bear so rare? Partly because its habitat is being destroyed. In Borneo and other parts of Malaysia, people can get rich by cutting down and selling hardwood trees. But trees are an important part of the sun bear's habitat. The bears climb trees and sleep in them during the day, and the trees provide food such as fruits and berries. Trees also create the right environment for prey such as birds, rodents, and insects.

Sun bears are further threatened by *poachers,* people who capture or kill animals illegally. Poachers usually can't capture adult sun bears because the animals are too aggressive. So they shoot the mother bears and take the cubs to sell as pets. The cubs are extremely sweet-natured and friendly. They suck their paws the way babies suck their thumbs. When the bears grow up, however, they lose their youthful charm and become quite aggressive.

Although it's against the law to shoot or capture sun bears, the laws are hard to enforce. And, of course, when a bear is hard to find, it becomes that much more desirable. The rarer the bear, the higher the price—and the higher the price, the more the poachers want it. It becomes a vicious circle.

Moon Bears

The sun bear gets its name from the golden-blond crescent that most of them have on their chest. In fact, however, that crescent looks more like a moon than a sun. Actually, it looks just like the crescent-shaped mark on an *Asian black bear,* commonly called the moon bear.

An average adult *moon bear* is built something like a short, stocky football player. It stands about 5 feet tall on its hind legs and weighs about 200 pounds. With shaggy fur on its shoulders and neck, the moon bear looks almost as if it's wearing someone else's coat.

Moon bears are twice the size of sun bears, but they are not nearly so rare. In fact, the moon bear has the opposite problem. In Japan there are so many moon bears that people are encouraged to hunt them. More than 2,000 are killed each year.

Why do people kill these appealing-looking animals? Moon bears are unpopular in Japan because they eat everything in sight: acorns, nuts, cherries, dogwoods, and lots of other little plants that are sending up new shoots. They also peel the bark from trees and chew on the juicy *sapwood,* the young, juicy layer underneath the bark. And as if that weren't enough, moon bears also are known for having a terrible temper. They're quick to attack people and horses. In Japan no one wants to save the moon bear.

Moon bears may not be endangered now, but if attitudes toward the bear don't change soon, its numbers may dwindle and it may eventually die out.

Spectacled Bear

Deep in the forests of the Andes Mountains of South America lives a beautiful shaggy black bear with golden markings on its face. It is called the *spectacled bear* because the markings look like eyeglasses. It is one of the rarest bears in the world. One wildlife researcher spent 7 years trying to find spectacled bears. In all that time he saw only eight of them.

An average adult of this species weighs between 250 and 350 pounds and stands about 5 feet tall. These bears survive mostly on plants and fruit, but they will eat prey animals such as mice, birds, and even domestic cattle if they're available. Great tree climbers, spectacled bears sometimes spend more time in the trees than they do on the ground.

The mountains and valleys of South America are the only places on earth where these bears are found. But, like many other previously unspoiled areas on earth, the spectacled bear's South American habitat is being destroyed as people move in.

Spectacled bears are also endangered because they are so often killed. Sometimes farmers kill the bears to keep them from eating their crops. Other times poachers are responsible for the deaths. They sell the bears to people who believe that certain parts of the bear are a good kind of medicine.

Sloth Bear

Meet the *sloth bear*. With its long, shaggy hair, it almost looks like a cross between a bear and an Old English Sheepdog! Of course, sloth bears are nothing like dogs, but then they aren't much like bears either. For one thing, sloth bears like to be with each other. Unlike grizzlies or giant pandas, sloth bears sometimes form families. For another thing, they aren't too aggressive. They aren't really predators. Usually a sloth bear will eat prey animals only if someone else does the killing.

Sloth bears live in the forests of India and Sri Lanka, where they can easily find their favorite food —termites. Their muzzles are specially designed to suck the termites out of their nests. The bears also love honey and will put up with countless bee stings just to get at a honeycomb.

Sloth bears were named after the sloth, a small, slow-moving mammal from South America that hangs upside down in trees. Although sloth bears are great climbers, they don't hang upside down. And they aren't always slow. Sometimes they even run or gallop. Their name is really not an accurate description of the sloth bear.

Can you guess what threatens the sloth bear's existence? The same condition that has endangered all other rare bears—cutting down the trees in their habitat. Sloth bears also unwittingly advertise their whereabouts to hunters. The noisy sucking sounds they make to extract termites from their nests can be heard up to 600 feet away. That's equal to 2 or 3 city blocks! These sounds let hunters know exactly where they are. So far, however, in spite of the outside threats, there are still about 8,000 sloth bears in the wild.

Someday the countries where these rare bears live may be able to protect them. In the meantime, zoos around the world are trying to save the bears by breeding them in captivity. In the United States there are breeding programs—and rare bears on display—in at least three places: the Brookfield Zoo in Chicago, the National Zoo in Washington, D.C., and the San Diego Zoo in California.

6

Famous Trained Bears

Everyone knows that movie stars can often be difficult. Sometimes they insist on fancy living quarters. Sometimes they don't show up on the film set on time. They often demand huge salaries, and when they're grouchy, they gripe and growl at the director and make everyone's life miserable.

But as film stars go, Bart was a pleasure. He was perfectly happy living in a simple trailer. He always reported to the set when he was needed. And his only extravagant demand was that he needed to eat 5 pounds of apples, 5 cans of salmon, 2 quarts of milk, 3 loaves of bread, and 6 chickens—each and every day!

Bart is the 9-foot 6-inch, 1,500-pound Kodiak bear who starred in the 1989 movie *The Bear*. Owned by Doug Seus, one of the best animal trainers in America, Bart has been performing in television commercials and low-budget movies for years. But *The Bear* was his first starring role and his most difficult part. For the movie, Bart, who is a male, had to learn to cuddle with a young cub named Douce. Such affectionate behavior is something that male bears never display in the wild. In fact, it's unheard of. Male brown bears have been known to kill cubs. Could Doug really teach Bart to do something that was so contrary to his instincts? If so, it would be a milestone in the world of bears.

A Bear's Teddy

To teach Bart to be gentle with Douce, Doug first taught the would-be star to be gentle with a teddy bear. Whenever Bart tried to bite or wrestle with the teddy, Doug would use a kind but firm voice to tell Bart, "No, no . . . *easy. Easy.*" But if Bart licked or kissed the teddy, Doug praised him, "Good boy! *Easy* kisses." Then he'd pet Bart and give him an apple.

Once Bart learned to treat the teddy bear with gentleness and "easy kisses," Doug introduced him to the real baby bear cub. Actually, Doug made the introductions in two steps. The first step was to let Bart and Douce get used to each other's scents. To do this, Doug put some of Douce's urine on the teddy bear. And he let Douce smell some of Bart's urine as well. Step two was the face-to-face meeting. Again, whenever Bart gently licked Douce, Doug gave the big bear a reward. "*Goooood* boy," Doug would say, drawing the words out affectionately. Then he petted Bart and gave him another apple.

Pet Bart? A hulking 1,500-pound grizzly bear? Absolutely, according to Doug Seus. Doug treats his animals with affection and respect. Unlike many animal trainers today and nearly all trainers of the past—

Doug doesn't use muzzles on his bears. "We have a relationship with our animals," he says. "That's the fun of it. I don't do this just for the money. I do it for the enjoyment of going out there to have a romp with them."

Males vs. Females

In addition to Bart, Doug has three other male bears that he romps with on his 10-acre property in Utah. Although male bears are naturally more aggressive than females, Doug prefers to work with males. He believes that their aggression can be turned into something positive. Males have a great deal of confidence, Doug says, and they pay attention better than females. He believes that females are always following their instincts to protect their young. As a result, they're always looking off to the sides, keeping a watch out for trouble. For a performing bear, who has to focus 100% of its attention on its act, that's not so good. "Males have a more riveting behavior," Doug says.

Doug has had a lot of success with male bears, but one of the earliest and most famous bear trainers of all time felt just the opposite. His name was Emil Pallenberg and he was born in Germany in the late 1800s. When he was 16 years old, Pallenberg decided that he wanted to train bears. Although he knew nothing about training animals, Emil saved his money, bought a bear, and set to work with his brothers, trying to teach the bear to ride a bicycle. All their training was done in the middle of the night at the zoo in Cologne because the Pallenbergs had to work at regular jobs during the day. When the bear refused to learn, Emil bought another bear, and then another. Soon he had so many bears that he couldn't afford to feed them.

But just when Pallenberg was about to give up, he found a bear with the right personality and willingness to learn. Her name was Ella, and she was the first bear ever to learn how to ride a bicycle. With Ella as the star, Emil and his brothers went on the road as a traveling circus act. From then on, Pallenberg worked only with females. In his prime, Pallenberg owned eight female bears that were trained not only to ride bicycles, but also to roller skate, play the concertina, dance with tiny dolls, and play the harmonica.

Bearly Balancing

How did Pallenberg teach Ella to ride a bike? It wasn't easy! He started with a *stationary,* or nonmovable, bicycle. Whenever Ella touched the bike, Emil praised her. Eventually, after many weeks, Ella learned how to put her paws on the handlebars. Months later Ella learned how to sit on the seat and put her back feet on the pedals. And finally she learned how to pedal. But the bike was still bolted in place.

Then came the hardest part. Pallenberg had to teach Ella how actually to balance and ride forward.

He used exactly the same technique that a parent uses to teach a young child to ride a bike. He held on to the bike to keep Ella steady, and ran along beside her as she pedaled. The only difference was that most 5-year-olds weigh about 40 or 50 pounds when they're learning to ride. Ella weighed close to 500!

Train or Tame?

Most experts agree that bears are extremely intelligent, and that makes them easy to train—but hard to tame. That is, they can learn and understand very quickly what is expected of them, but they don't necessarily want to cooperate. And the one thing that all animal trainers seem to agree on is that bears are more dangerous than lions or tigers. In fact, bears are the most aggressive, most dangerous wild animals in the world.

Doug Seus knows how dangerous bears are. But because he uses methods that respect the bear's intelligence, he's very successful. He says that once he has established a *rapport,* or relationship, with an animal, he can teach it to perform a new behavior with just ten repetitions. For instance, for the movie *The Bear,* Doug had to teach Bart to limp. Newspaper and magazine articles reported that it took 2 years for Bart to learn that trick. But in truth, Doug says it took only 3 days!

Doug considers his bears very tame. But Jean-Jacques Annaud, the director of *The Bear,* probably wouldn't agree. During the filming, Doug used lightly electrified wires to mark off Bart's territory. Bart knew that he wasn't supposed to cross those wires— but the rule worked both ways. Neither were people on the film crew supposed to invade Bart's territory. At the end of the filming, Annaud, without thinking, stepped into Bart's area to pose for publicity photos —and Bart attacked. He knocked Annaud to the ground and left a deep impression on the director: claw marks in his backside. It was just a small reminder to everyone involved that bears are not people. No matter how intelligent, well-trained, or affectionate they may seem, they will attack when they feel threatened.

7

Coming Too Close

It was a beautiful, warm Memorial Day morning in 1991 when two joggers were out for their early morning run in Camarillo, California. Suddenly they spotted a black bear. A bear in a nice, civilized California suburb? Weird, they thought. What's it doing here?

The answer was simple. The bear was heading for McDonald's! Its keen nose had told it that there was food somewhere within walking distance, so down from the mountains the bear came. When McDonald's turned out to be closed (and their garbage unavailable), the bear ambled on to a Mexican restaurant down the road.

Fortunately, that restaurant wasn't open either. It was too early—5:30 A.M.!—so no one was around. And luckily the joggers had called the police. Soon the bear was shot with a tranquilizer dart and carted off to the mountains where it belonged. No one got hurt in the encounter.

Sometimes it turns out that way. Bears come too close to human beings—and nothing bad happens. That's lucky for both the people and the bears. Why lucky for the bears? Because when people are threatened or injured by bears, the bears have to be removed. Usually, that means transporting the nuisance animals to a distant area. But if the bear is a repeated and distinct threat to people, it may have to be killed.

Dinner for One

Take the incident in Wyoming in August 1990, for example. A large group of vacationers had signed up and paid for a special treat. They were to ride on horseback into Yellowstone National Park and have a cookout. But halfway through the steak dinner, a grizzly bear appeared. What a treat for a bear—steaks! Instantly all 180 people jumped up and fled. They let the bear have what it had come for—dinner for one. Immediately the bear began to eat—all 180 portions of steak. And before it was finished, it had also eaten 180 servings of cole slaw, watermelon, and baked beans, too.

This particular bear was a *yearling,* an animal that is a year old, so it weighed only about 170 pounds. Park officials think it may have learned about raiding campsites from its mother. She was also a nuisance bear and had been removed from the park a few months earlier and sent to Washington State. After the steak attack, her cub was tranquilized and relocated to a distant area of Yellowstone.

It may sound funny to hear about a bear raiding a cookout and eating everyone's food. But park officials don't laugh about grizzly bear encounters with people. Not everyone is so lucky as the 180 vacationers who lost only their meal. Every once in a while a bear finds another way to have a massive dinner for one—by attacking and eating a human being.

That's what happened to Jay B. L. Reeves. He was a 38-year-old wildlife photographer who went to Frosty Creek in Alaska to shoot pictures of bears. Jay planned to camp out alone in the woods for a week. But sometime during his first night there, he was attacked and eaten by a bear. No one knows exactly what happened. All that is known is that the photographer made two serious mistakes. One: He kept food in his tent. And two: He camped where bears were likely to find him—on a bear trail near a large salmon stream.

Why Do Bears Attack?

People have been attacked and mauled by bears for many reasons. Usually, the attacks fall into one of the following categories:

- The bear feels threatened or surprised.
- A mother bear is protecting her cubs. Females with cubs will defend their babies to the death.
- The bear charges because the person tries to run.
- The bear is hungry, having just come out of its winter den.
- The bear is a *subadult,* sort of a "teenager" bear. Subadult male bears are often more aggressive

than adult males. They're at an age when they some-times attack just to show how tough they are.

- The bear is a known killer. This category is the scariest and is based on the belief that once a bear tastes a human, it will kill again. Another theory maintains that a bear will turn mean if it has been shot at and wounded by a person. As a result, it develops a hatred toward all people and becomes aggressive. Since bears are known for having an excellent memory, this may be true. Another theory is that bears never forget where they had a good meal.

But in spite of all the stories, remember this: Most of the time bears don't attack people. Most meetings between bears and people end the way they should—with *no one* getting hurt. If a bear can walk away from a meeting with a human without losing face, it usually will.

How to Protect Yourself

The following advice is given by rangers and guides to campers and hikers who might encounter bears:

- *Don't travel alone.*
- *Never run.* A bear can always outrun you. And bears are drawn to attack when they see a person or animal in flight. No matter how fast you run, a grizzly bear—even if it's 150 feet away—can catch you before you've taken 10 steps. They run up to 35 miles per hour. Most other bears are fast, too.
- *Don't scream or yell, and don't stare at the bear.*

In the animal world, staring is a sign of aggression. Just look away and talk quietly. Give the bear a chance to walk away. You might also want to back up *slowly,* to let the bear know that you don't intend to attack it.

- *Try not to show fear.* Bears respect people until the person does something to change that respect. Even if the bear stands up to sniff you, don't panic. People think that that's how bears attack—by walking toward you with their paws outstretched. But that's not true. A bear on its hind legs is usually only trying to scare you. When a bear really wants to charge, it will drop down on all fours. But even that doesn't necessarily mean you are going to be attacked. Sometimes a bear bluffs. It charges, then turns away at the last minute. So stay calm and try not to move.

- *Try to determine whether it's a black bear or a brown bear.* (Chapter 2 gives tips on how to tell them apart.) Then act accordingly. Black bears will often run and hide if they can find a good escape route. But some black bears have been known to attack people with the intention of eating them. So the best advice with black bears is to do nothing unless the bear actually attacks. Then and only then, fight back as hard as you can. Don't play dead with a black bear, because it may just keep on attacking. Black bears can be discouraged if you punch them or kick them hard, but that's not the case with grizzlies.

Grizzlies and other brown bears are just the opposite. They almost never run if they feel threatened. A grizzly would rather stay and fight. On the other hand, a grizzly bear is more likely to stop attacking if you play dead. Again, do nothing unless the grizzly actually charges you and makes contact. Then fall to the ground and remain motionless until you are sure that the bear is gone.

• *Consider carrying bear repellent.* One brand, called *Counter Assault,* comes in a spray can. It contains a red pepper oil that will irritate the bear's eyes for about 5 or 10 minutes—long enough for you to get away.

Most of all, try to remember that most bears are not bad animals. They aren't out to "get" you. Most of them are just minding their own business in a habitat that originally belonged to them.